This Journal Belongs To:

www.ingramcontent.com/pod-product-compliance
Lightning Source LLC
Chambersburg PA
CBHW020322290526
45785CB00007B/2890